MARTIN LUTHER KING JR.

JEAN DARBY

In Consultation with Martha Cosgrove,
M.A. and Reading Specialist

JUST THE FACTS BIOGRAPHIES

LERNER PUBLICATIONS COMPANY/MINNEAPOLIS

Martha Cosgrove has a master's degree from the University of Minnesota in secondary education, with an emphasis on developmental and remedial reading. She is licensed in 7–12 English and language arts, developmental reading, and remedial reading. She has had several works published, and she gives numerous state and national presentations in her areas of expertise.

Lerner Publications Company
A division of Lerner Publishing Group
241 First Avenue North
Minneapolis, Minnesota U.S.A.

Website address: www.lernerbooks.com

Library of Congress Cataloging-in-Publication Data

Darby, Jean, 1921–
    Martin Luther King Jr. / by Jean Darby.
        p.   cm. – (Just the facts biographies)
    Includes bibliographical references and index.
    ISBN: 0–8225–2471–6 (lib. bdg. : alk. paper)
    1. King, Martin Luther, Jr., 1929–1968–Juvenile literature. 2. African Americans–Biography–Juvenile literature. 3. Baptists–United States– Clergy–Biography–Juvenile literature. 4. Civil rights workers–United States–Biography–Juvenile literature. 5. African Americans–Civil rights– History–20th century–Juvenile literature. 6. Nonviolence–Religious aspects–Baptists–Juvenile literature. I. Title. II. Series.
    E185.97.K5D29 2005
    323'.092–dc22   2004027791

Manufactured in the United States of America
1 2 3 4 5 6 – JR – 10 09 08 07 06 05

CONTENTS

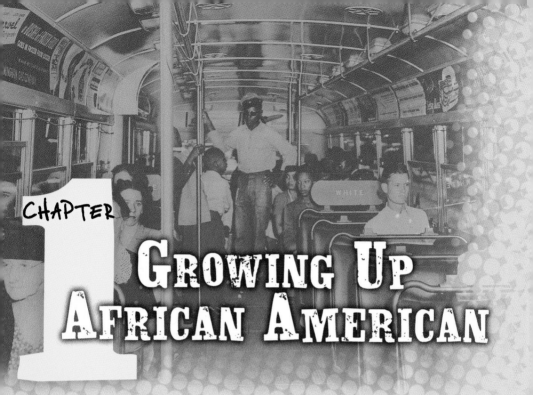

CHAPTER 1
GROWING UP AFRICAN AMERICAN

(Above) A segregated bus in the southern United States during the 1950s. Southern segregation laws separated African Americans and whites.

EARLY IN HIS LIFE, young Martin Luther King Jr. learned about racial prejudice. The story goes that one sunny day, Martin skipped across the street to play with his friends, who were the sons of the neighborhood grocer. When he knocked on the door, he stood and waited longer than usual for someone to answer. His friends' mother finally answered, but she looked at him in a strange way. Her voice sounded different as she told him he was too old to play with her sons.

4

Martin hurried home to his own mother. He was confused by the change in the way his friends' mother treated him. Martin's mother knelt down and hugged him. She explained that he was as good as anyone else but that many people didn't think African Americans were as good as whites. Martin's friends were white. Their mother didn't want her sons playing with an African American boy anymore.

Martin soon learned to read signs that said, "No Colored Allowed" and "Whites Only." This separation, or segregation, of people based on race is a form of racial discrimination.

Martin also learned about racial prejudice when he went shopping with his mother. One day, when Martin and his mother were in a store, he saw an elevator with fancy trim and buttons. He wanted to ride the elevator, but his mother told him it was just for white people. Instead, they rode a bigger elevator that also carried boxes and crates. It wasn't nearly as exciting as the elevator Martin had seen. Another time, a white woman yelled that Martin had stepped on her toe. She slapped Martin across the face. Martin started to wonder what was wrong with being African American.

Little did he know that he'd spend his life fighting against racial prejudice. Little did he know that he'd give his life for the cause of winning freedom and equality for all.

EARLY DAYS

Martin Luther King Jr. came quietly into the world on January 15, 1929. He was the second child of Alberta and Martin Luther King Sr. When he was born, he was so still that the doctor thought he wouldn't live. But after several strong slaps on his bottom, he started crying.

The King family—which included a daughter Christine and later another son A. D.—lived in a gray and white house in downtown Atlanta, Georgia. Martin's family was respected in Atlanta's African American community. Martin Sr. was a Baptist minister, who preached about the worth

IT'S A FACT!

Martin was born under the name Michael Luther King, which was also his father's name. When the boy was about six, his father decided to rename himself and his son Martin Luther King. Martin Luther was a famous German religious reformer of the 1500s.

Jim Crow laws in the South said that public places for African Americans and whites were to be separate but equal. Places for African Americans, such as this movie theater, were separate but usually not equal.

of African American people. He told the people in his church to be strong and brave. He tried to protect his daughter and two sons from the insults and abuses that African Americans often suffered at the time, but it was not always possible.

Georgia is part of the South. In the 1930s, many southern states had laws to separate the races. They were called Jim Crow laws. African Americans couldn't eat where white people ate or go to the same movie theaters. They had to eat at "colored" restaurants. They had to go to separate theaters, where they watched old, faded films.

African American children had to attend separate schools, which were run down and poorly equipped. They couldn't drink from the same water fountains as whites or buy sodas where white children bought theirs. African Americans also had to ride in the back of the city buses. In some places they couldn't ride on a city bus at all.

As Martin grew older, he also grew angrier and angrier at how African Americans in Georgia were treated. His father worked hard to set a good example of self-esteem. Once, Martin and his father went into a shoe store and sat in the chairs near the door. The clerk told them they couldn't sit there. Martin's father told the clerk that if he couldn't sit in the chairs, he wouldn't buy any shoes. They left the store.

FAMILY LIFE

Martin had a good life at home. He lived in a middle-class family. He never suffered from hunger or cold. He had plenty of warm clothes and good food. He enjoyed sports, such as baseball and basketball. He lived in a nice house. And best of all, Jennie Williams, his beloved grandmother, lived in the same house.

Martin also loved Ebenezer Baptist Church, where his father preached and where Martin studied the Bible. During church services, he sat in the family pew with his grandmother, his sister Christine, and his brother A.D. From there, Martin looked up at his father, who sat in a tall wooden chair in front of a gold cross. His mother sat at the organ and played music for the service. The worship service was loud and lively, with people singing, clapping hands, and dancing. Martin's father was a good speaker, and his words often caused people to cry with joy.

IT'S A FACT!
Jennie Williams, called Mama, was the mother of Martin's mother. When Jennie's husband died in 1931, she moved in with Martin and his family. Martin quickly became her favorite grandchild. He, in turn, loved her dearly.

After the Sunday worship service, the church held a Sunday dinner. Tables were filled with fried chicken, ham, black-eyed peas, and watermelon. When Martin was only six, he sang hymns at these gatherings.

People who knew Martin realized that he was not an ordinary child. He began reading at an early age. His favorite books were about African American history and the people who made it.

He read about Frederick Douglass and Harriet Tubman. Both had been slaves who had escaped to freedom in the 1800s. He read about Booker T. Washington, who started the first college for African Americans in Alabama, another southern state. And he learned how George Washington Carver researched and developed many products from peanuts. Stretched out on his bed, Martin read stories of singer Paul Robeson, of boxer Joe Louis, and of runner Jesse Owens. In 1936, Owens had won four gold medals at the Summer Olympic Games. Martin was such a good student that he skipped ninth grade and caught up with his sister Christine, who was a year older.

NEW HORIZONS

A worldwide war started in 1939, when Martin was only ten years old. The United States entered World War II (1939–1945) in 1941. Many young men joined the U.S. Army and the U.S. Navy. With these men off to war, some colleges didn't have enough male students to fill their classrooms. So they invited gifted high school students to attend. In 1944, when Martin was only fifteen, he passed a college entrance exam. He'd start classes at Morehouse College in Atlanta in the fall of that year.

But first, he'd see another part of the United States. During summer 1944, before he entered Morehouse full-time, he and his brother worked in the northeastern state of Connecticut picking tobacco. This is the leafy plant that goes into making cigarettes. Several high school and college students were in the group. Most of the students worked in Connecticut because they wanted to see what life was like in a different part of the country. It was a happy time for Martin. In Connecticut and other northern states, laws didn't separate the races as they did in the South.

In Connecticut, Martin didn't have to worry about segregation. He could eat where his white friends ate. He could ride in the front of the bus if he wanted to. African Americans and whites used the same restrooms. No "Whites Only" signs were anywhere.

In many ways, Martin was a normal teenager. He liked nice clothes, and his friends called him

MOREHOUSE COLLEGE

Morehouse College started in 1867 as a place where young African American men could be trained for teaching and for ministering in the Baptist Church. Since its founding, the college has expanded many, many times. Morehouse offers degrees in economics, engineering, science, mathematics, and theology. The college has earned an international reputation for training scholars and leaders from around the world.

The Morehouse College campus in the late 1800s

Tweed after a type of fabric. He liked girls and loved loud music. He also liked to dance, an activity that got him into trouble with his father. Martin Sr. didn't approve of dancing. When he learned that his son had been attending dances, he made Martin apologize in front of all the worshippers at Ebenezer Baptist Church.

But Martin was serious too. At Morehouse College, he soon came to believe that white people were not the problem in the South. The problem was racial segregation. Even though he was still quite young, Martin decided that all people were equal. He believed that people of all races should be able to live in the same neighborhoods, work together on the same jobs, and use the same drinking fountains, hotels, and restaurants.

Martin enjoyed talking about these issues with professors and other students at Morehouse. The discussions made him wonder what he should do with his future.

Martin lived at home while he went to college. At first, Martin told his father that he was thinking of becoming a lawyer or a doctor. But later, he met two Morehouse ministers, Dr. George D. Kelsey, director of the religion department, and Dr. Benjamin E. Mays, the college president. These men had a great influence on him. By his third year of college, Martin had decided to become a minister too. He was ready to devote his life to the Baptist Church.

In 1948, nineteen-year-old Martin graduated with a bachelor of arts degree from Morehouse College. He immediately enrolled in Crozer Theological Seminary in Chester, Pennsylvania.

At this school, he'd pursue further studies to become a minister. He'd also be living alone for the first time. He'd be away from the powerful influence of his father.

In his new school, Martin tried to overcome white people's stereotypes, or set ideas, of African Americans. He believed that whites thought that African Americans were always late, loud, laughing, and messy. Martin didn't want to fall into any of these stereotypes. As a result, Martin was overly serious. He dressed with extreme care and was always very neat. If he was even a minute late for class, he thought everyone noticed.

Martin took his studying seriously, attending classes during the day and studying late into the night. He learned about some of the world's great thinkers and activists. Activists work actively for a cause in which they believe. Martin wanted to be an activist and work to make the world a better place for all people. At Crozer, he began looking for a way to do this.

In 1950, Martin went to a talk by Dr. Mordecai Johnson. Dr. Johnson was president of Howard University—a college in Washington, D.C., for African American students. Dr. Johnson had

India's Mohandas Gandhi *(front left)* leads a march to peacefully protest unfair British laws during the 1930s. Martin was moved by Gandhi's nonviolent approach to injustice.

just returned from India. He talked about his travels and about the spiritual leadership of a man named Mohandas Gandhi. Martin knew a little about Gandhi's lifelong work to help free India from British rule. The British had governed India for hundreds of years. Instead of fighting the British with guns, Gandhi and his supporters had used a different method called nonviolent resistance. They took part in hunger fasts, where people refused to eat for days and weeks. They had boycotts, refusing to buy British goods. Workers went on strike, staying home from their jobs. None of these activities was violent. But all of them showed how much the people of India resisted British rule.

Gandhi also helped to organize peaceful protest marches. He preached the idea of openly disobeying certain laws and willingly facing the penalty for doing so. Martin was impressed with Gandhi's methods. But he was not sure that these techniques would work to fight racial prejudice in the United States.

IT'S A FACT!

As a reward for hard work and excellence in school, Martin's parents gave him a brand-new, green Chevrolet car.

In 1951, Martin graduated from Crozer with the highest grade point average in his class. He won the Plafker Award as most outstanding student. He also received the J. Lewis Crozer fellowship, which gave him the money to study at a university of his choice.

BECOMING DR. KING

The next September, at the age of twenty-two, Martin entered Boston University in Boston, Massachusetts, as a graduate student in philosophy. He continued to study the works of the great thinkers he had first learned about at Crozer.

CORETTA SCOTT KING

Coretta Scott was born in Alabama and worked hard to do well in school. In 1945, she earned a scholarship to go to Antioch College in Yellow Springs, Ohio. She majored in music and education. Meanwhile, she also joined civil rights groups, including the local chapter of the National Association for the Advancement of Colored People (NAACP). In 1951, she got another scholarship to study music at the New England Conservatory in Boston. She intended to become a concert singer. While there, she met Martin Luther King Jr.

With every page he read, Martin's curiosity grew. He was alert, eager, strong, and restless. He studied at Boston University during the day and drove to nearby Harvard University to attend extra classes at night.

Martin was bright and good-looking. He wanted to meet a woman who was intelligent, with a strong character and a good personality. Martin found what he was looking for in a music student at the New England Conservatory of Music in Boston. Her name was Coretta Scott. He asked her for a date. Scott didn't intend to marry a ministry student. She pictured herself traveling across the country on concert tours, performing before audiences.

She didn't want to give up that life to be a minister's wife, but as the couple dated, they fell in love. On June 18, 1953, the couple was married in Marion, Alabama, Coretta's hometown. After their honeymoon, the couple moved into an apartment in Boston near the conservatory.

Soon after the wedding, Martin finished the classes he needed for his degree. He accepted a job as a minister at Dexter Avenue Baptist Church in Montgomery, Alabama. Martin traveled to Montgomery on weekends and returned to Boston, where Coretta was still in school, during the week.

After living comfortably in the North, the Kings did not want to return to the South. But Martin felt that he

Martin and Coretta during the 1950s. The couple moved back to the South and its system of segregation in 1953.

was needed there. He told Coretta that they would stay only a short time.

In the summer of 1955, Martin earned his doctorate degree (Ph.D) in theology (religion) and became Dr. Martin Luther King Jr. It was an exciting day for the King family. At the time, few African American people earned such high degrees. Martin felt satisfied that his life was moving forward. He was gaining knowledge and respect.

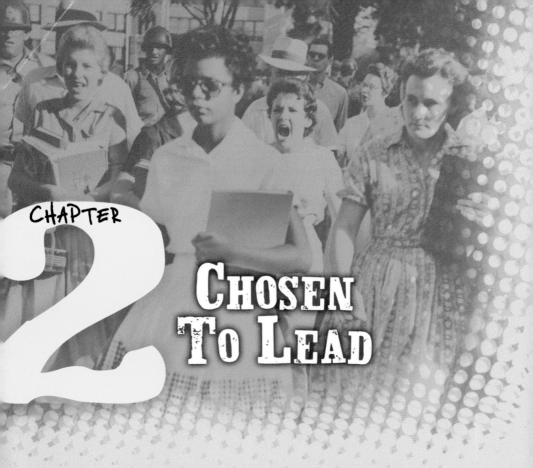

CHAPTER 2
CHOSEN TO LEAD

In 1954, the U.S. Supreme Court—the nation's highest court—ruled that public schools were to be desegregated. The court made a ruling in a case called *Brown v.* (against) *the Board of Education*. The court said African American students and white students should go to school together. Many white southerners were shocked. Some people spoke out against the decision in newspapers, on radio and television, and to their government leaders.

THE *BROWN* CASE

The desegregation decision was part of a famous legal case. The case was called *Brown v. the Board of Education of Topeka* (Kansas). It started when Oliver Brown, an African American, challenged the view that his daughter could not go to a white school near their family home in Topeka.

The NAACP decided to use the *Brown* case to change the laws that kept African Americans and whites from going to the same schools. These laws kept to a view that schools could be "separate but equal." The NAACP argued—and the U.S. Supreme Court agreed—that separate schools could never be equal. The decision said all public schools had to be desegregated. While the process got started in the mid-1950s, it was a long time before desegregation was completed.

They worried that people of different races would begin to marry and have families together. Groups that violently opposed desegregation were called White Citizens Councils. These groups sprang up in the South.

At first, the Court's decision had little effect in Montgomery. African American and white children continued to go to separate schools. But pressure continued to grow. African Americans were tired of being put down. They were tired of riding in the back of buses and of being insulted by white people.

They were tired of cruel and unfair treatment. They'd had enough of segregation.

ROSA GETS MARTIN INVOLVED

In 1955, on an unusually warm December day in Montgomery, Alabama, Rosa Parks took a step that changed everything. Tired after a long day at work, Rosa climbed on a bus to go home from her job at a department store. She boarded the bus and found a seat just behind the white section.

When the bus pulled up to the Empire Theater stop, six white people got on. The bus driver, J. F. Blake, asked some of the African American riders to give up their seats for the white passengers. The practice was common and happened every day. Three African American passengers stood up right away, but Rosa didn't move. Blake again asked Rosa to give up her seat, and again she refused. She sat motionless. She had made up her mind. She was going to stay seated.

The driver called the police. Rosa was charged with breaking the city bus rules. But her act had gotten a great deal of public attention. Many people were angry that she had been charged with a crime just for sitting in her seat.

A police officer fingerprints Rosa Parks. She was arrested for refusing to obey segregated busing laws in Montgomery, Alabama, on December 1, 1955.

Rosa's case was what African American leaders had been waiting for. They took her case to court to test the bus law. The case helped to show how bad the laws in the South were for African Americans. At the police station, Rosa was able to call a leader in the African American community. She called E. D. Nixon, who arranged for her release. News of Parks's arrest spread quickly.

Throughout the African American community, people talked about her story.

ORGANIZING THE BOYCOTT

On Friday, December 2, about forty-five ministers and civic leaders, including Martin Luther King, called a meeting. The group decided to organize a boycott against the Montgomery city bus company. All the African Americans in Montgomery would refuse to ride the buses. This boycott would cost the bus company most of its business. Soon the company would lose money and be forced to make new rules that were fair to all. They thought this nonviolent action would send a strong message.

For the boycott work, all the African Americans in Montgomery would have to know about it and be willing to work together. The leaders knew the boycott would bring hardship to many people who needed to ride buses. But they also thought it would bring power to the African American community.

By late Friday afternoon, leaflets had been printed and passed out. They told people not to ride buses on Monday, December 5. The leaflets told people to find other rides, take cabs, or walk to wherever they needed to go.

JO ANN ROBINSON

Jo Ann Robinson was an African American college professor and a member of the Women's Political Council in Montgomery. Soon after hearing the news of Parks's arrest, Robinson printed the handouts that urged African Americans to boycott the buses on Monday. She and her students gave out the leaflets beginning Friday morning. Ministers discussed the boycott in their Sunday sermons. By Monday, empty buses rolled throughout the city.

King wasn't sure the boycott was a good idea. The bus drivers might lose their jobs if the boycott was a success. Families of bus workers depended on the money they earned. King read books and prayed, searching for answers to these problems. After a great deal of thought, King decided that the boycott was not intended to hurt anyone. The African American community would simply be refusing to cooperate with an unfair system. He could go along with that idea.

Most African Americans in Montgomery welcomed the news of the boycott, but the boycott leaders wondered if they would really support it. The weather on Monday morning might be cold or rainy. People might decide it was too hard to walk or to find another ride.

People encouraged each other to take part,
but they could not hide their fear. On Sunday,
the upcoming boycott got front-page coverage
in the city newspaper, the *Montgomery Advertiser.*
African American ministers preached about it in
church that day and talked about the need for
loyalty and sacrifice.

THE BOYCOTT BEGINS

Coretta and Martin awoke earlier than usual on
Monday morning. At 5:30 A.M., they were dressed
and waiting to see the first bus pass their window at
6:00 A.M. Martin went into the kitchen to make a
cup of coffee. In the living room, Coretta watched
for the bus to come down the hill. They wondered
if it would be full. Finally, the bus appeared.

Coretta called to her husband. Martin put down
his coffee and ran to the living room. They leaned
forward, peering through the window. An empty bus
passed by. Martin jumped into his car and drove
down every major street to watch each passing bus.
Throughout the city, he saw only eight passengers.
Some people rode mules. Others drove horse-drawn
buggies. People with cars shared rides. Hundreds of
people walked to show their commitment.

King wasn't sure Montgomery's African American community would go through with the bus boycott. He was pleased to see empty buses on the first day of the boycott.

Some white people were surprised by the determination of the African American community. They said the community was forcing people away from the buses. But it wasn't true. The African American people were united. The boycott was on.

At 9:00 A.M., Dr. Martin Luther King and his friend, the Reverend Ralph Abernathy, pastor of the First Baptist Church, drove to city hall to attend Rosa Parks's trial. She had told the court that she was not guilty of the charge of breaking the bus law.

A trial was the only way to decide who was right. A crowd had gathered, filling the streets and sidewalks. Police stood guard. Martin worried that violence might break out.

People waited for the verdict, or court's decision. When the guilty verdict was announced, many people were angry. Rosa Parks was fined ten dollars plus the costs of going on trial. The court said she had broken the bus law. But her lawyer, Fred Gray, immediately filed an appeal. This was a legal request for the court to reconsider its decision. Usually, a court with broader powers hears the appeal. The segregation law would be tested in this higher court.

People around the country wondered why Rosa Parks had remained seated on that day. She was no more tired that day than usual. She was just

IT'S A FACT!

Ralph Abernathy—also a Baptist minister in Alabama—was one of Martin's closest friends. Together, they set up the bus boycott in Montgomery. They also founded the Southern Christian Leadership Conference (SCLC). Abernathy served as the SCLC's vice president.

tired of unfair treatment. Segregation was finally under attack, and Martin Luther King was ready to lead the charge.

THE BOYCOTT CONTINUES

The one-day boycott had been a success. But the boycott leaders had to decide whether to continue it. Summer days would be hot, and winter days would be cold and windy. They wondered if people would get tired of the boycott and start riding the buses again.

They quickly decided to continue the boycott. They formed an organization called the Montgomery Improvement Association (MIA). Martin Luther King was elected president. The group wanted to continue the boycott until a few basic demands were met. They demanded courteous treatment by bus drivers. They wanted the seats to be available on a first-come, first-served basis. They also wanted the bus company to hire African Americans to drive the buses that served mostly African American neighborhoods.

Before they closed the meeting, the members of the MIA decided King should give a speech at a large meeting that evening. Held at a local church, this meeting would be open to the public. King, Parks, and others would tell the African American community to continue the boycott.

On the way home, King wondered how Coretta would accept his new responsibility. He didn't need to worry. She told him she was on his side. King's obligations were growing at home as well as in the community. His first child–Yolanda Denise, nicknamed Yoki–was just two weeks old.

That evening, King drove slowly into the area where the mass meeting was to take place. Police cars circled the church to stop any disturbance. Hundreds of people were outside, unable to get inside because the church was already full.

Afraid that he was late, he hurried toward the church. Four thousand people were standing outside when he arrived. He could hear the voices of men, women, and children whispering in excitement. Then over the top of the crowd, through a loudspeaker, he could hear the people inside the church singing. The church was packed, and the crowd cheered loudly as he entered. When Rosa Parks told her story, the crowd cheered again.

Then Martin Luther King Jr. stepped to the podium. His voice was clear and intense. He spoke

On the evening of December 5, 1955, King gave a speech to Montgomery's African American community *(above)*. He asked the community to continue its boycott until city buses were desegregated.

from his heart. He said that African Americans were tired of being treated unfairly. He told them it was time for a change. But he also told them that the African American people of Montgomery would not use violence or fear to reach their goals. He said that love and faith would be their weapons.

When Martin finished speaking, people inside
and outside cheered. They waved their hands,
stamped their feet, and thanked God. When the
applause finally quieted, Ralph Abernathy stepped
forward. He read the requirements to end the
boycott and asked all those in favor to stand. Every
person in the hall stood. They agreed to stay off
the buses until all of their demands were met.

When King finished his speech on December 5, 1955, the
crowd cheered. They fully supported continuing the
Montgomery bus boycott.

CHAPTER 3

LEADING THE BOYCOTT

MARTIN LUTHER KING and the MIA worked hard to make the boycott a success. They made plans to help seventeen thousand daily bus riders get where they needed to go every day. African American-owned taxi companies agreed not to charge more than ten cents, which was the cost of a bus ride at that time.

Montgomery's white police commissioner Clyde Sellers decided to end cheap taxi fares. He ordered the taxis to charge forty-five cents, hoping that when people couldn't afford taxis, they would return to the buses. But his idea didn't work. The African American people of Montgomery continued the boycott.

King, Abernathy, and other MIA leaders also organized a car pool, where African Americans could share rides. Many wealthy African American people, who ordinarily did not ride the buses, volunteered their cars. Doctors, lawyers, and business owners put in long hours as drivers. Soon the MIA opened an office of ten people to keep the car pool effort going.

IT'S A FACT!

More than one hundred people offered their vehicles for the car pools. Some drivers drove all day long. But many people chose to walk, even though car pools were available. Walking became a symbol of protest in Montgomery.

The media carried news of the boycott across the country and throughout the world. Donations began to arrive from around the United States, as well as other countries, such as Japan, India, Britain, and France. By March 1956, the MIA had raised sixty-five thousand dollars and was able to buy fifteen station wagons for the car pool. And still, many African American people continued to walk.

African American citizens of Montgomery, Alabama, walk rather than take buses during the bus boycott. King told boycotters that it was better to walk with pride than to put up with segregation.

MONTGOMERY'S WHITES RESPOND

Some Montgomery whites believed in the boycott. Three white people even helped with the car pool. But most other whites were angry and afraid. They had not been prepared for the determination of the African American community. Some whites wondered what was happening to society. They weren't just worried about losing seats on the bus. They sensed that they were losing their power, and that scared them.

A police officer tickets a car pool driver during the Montgomery bus boycott. The police targeted car pools of boycotters to force African Americans back to city buses.

The White Citizens Council came up with an idea. They would take away the licenses of the car pool drivers and cancel their insurance. Without licenses and insurance, these people wouldn't be able to legally drive. The police department in Montgomery also harassed and arrested drivers who gave rides to African American people. They gave tickets for blocking traffic, speeding, loitering, and for every imaginable reason.

One evening in 1956, King was driving home when two police officers pulled him over. One of the police officers leaned over King's window and told him that he was under arrest for speeding.

The officers made him get into a patrol car. King was scared as he sat in the car. They weren't going toward town. They were headed in the opposite direction. They were moving into an area controlled by the Ku Klux Klan. This racist group often beat or hanged African Americans without anyone knowing what had happened to the Klan's victims.

THE KU KLUX KLAN

After the Civil War (1861–1865), white southern soldiers founded the Ku Klux Klan as a secret society. Its aim was to stop African Americans and other minority groups from voting or using their other civil rights to achieve equal treatment. Violence and terror were the tools Klan members used. They beat or murdered African Americans in many parts of the South. Klan members wore white hoods to hide themselves *(right)*.

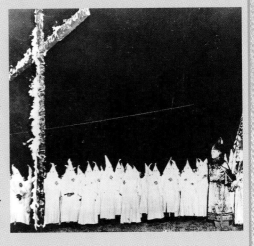

The Klan violently opposed the civil rights activities of the 1950s and 1960s. They targeted major civil rights activists, such as King and Abernathy, as well as others who were trying to gain equal rights for all Americans. The Klan also went after citizens who took part in the civil rights movement.

The driver turned onto a dark street that went under a bridge. King felt his heart pounding. He wondered if the men were really police. He worried they might kill him. He was shaking when he saw a sign that read Montgomery Jail. King was relieved that he was safe, but it was the first time he had been locked behind bars.

News of his arrest spread quickly. Soon an angry crowd gathered in front of the jail. The police didn't want to let King go, even though Ralph Abernathy tried to organize his release.

Outside, the crowd continued to grow. Inside, the police were getting nervous as they wondered what the crowd might do. They decided they'd better let King go.

King's first arrest was during the Montgomery bus boycott. Police charged him with speeding and tried to scare him into ending the protest. He was later charged with organizing an illegal boycott.

Not long after his arrest, King was speaking at a large meeting when he learned that his house had been bombed. He jumped from the platform and hurried out the side door. By the time he reached home, more than three hundred angry African Americans had already gathered. The men were armed with guns, clubs, rocks, and knives. The crowd was not going to move.

King pushed his way through to find his family. They were safe. Coretta explained that she had heard a noise on the front porch. She had gone to the back of the house, where Yoki was sleeping. When the bomb exploded, it sounded as though the whole front of the house had been blown away. Luckily, the bomb only split a pillar on the porch and broke the front windows. The living room was filled with broken glass and smoke. Soon the house was filled with police officers and firefighters. Mayor W. A. "Tacky" Gayle and the police commissioner were also there.

After talking with Coretta for a few minutes, King stepped out on the porch to face the shouting, cursing crowd. He was a respected leader in Montgomery's African American community. Someone wanted to hurt him and his young family.

King calms an angry African American crowd from his front porch following a bombing of his home in 1956.

The city could have been the scene of a fierce and bloody riot, but Martin Luther King showed the world what kind of man he was. He raised his arms and told the crowd not to take violent action. He told them to love their enemies and to pray for them.

With his words, King became a living symbol. His house had just been badly damaged. The lives of his wife and child had been threatened. But still, he preached love and forgiveness.

THE COURTS DECIDE

On November 13, 1956, King and the civil rights movement received good news. The U.S. Supreme Court had just ruled that Alabama's state and local laws requiring segregation on buses were unconstitutional.

The following night, members of the Ku Klux Klan pulled their white hoods over their heads. They piled into forty cars and rode up and down the streets of Montgomery to terrify the city's African American citizens. Ordinarily, threats of Klan violence were a signal for African Americans to stay in their homes, pull down their shades, and turn off the lights. This time, with new courage, they stood openly on porches as if they were watching a parade. Some even waved at the passing cars. Others ignored the cars. The Klan members quickly grew tired and went home.

But the White Citizens Council threatened violence if the order was enforced. On December 18, the city commissioners issued a statement saying that it would continue to fight segregation.

On the morning of December 21, 1956, more than a year after the boycott began. King, Ralph Abernathy, E. D. Nixon, and the Reverend Glenn Smiley, a white minister, rode on Montgomery's first integrated bus.

But the battle wasn't over. The White Citizens Council and the Klan carried through on their promises of violence. An African American teenage

Victory! King (second row, left) and other boycotters ride one of Montgomery's first desegregated buses in December 1956. The U.S. Supreme Court struck down Alabama's segregated busing laws in November that year.

girl was dragged from her home and beaten. A pregnant African American woman was shot in the leg. An outbreak of bombings hit African American homes and businesses. Abernathy's house was bombed, and King found a bundle of dynamite on his front porch one night.

Because of the violence, buses stopped running for a while. But city officials and business leaders finally decided to step in. Seven white men were arrested for the violence. An all-white jury found them not guilty, even with signed confessions from the men. Still, it was important that the men had gone to trial. It sent a message that Montgomery wouldn't accept racial violence. After the trial, the violence in Montgomery declined. The buses started running again.

With the success of the yearlong boycott, King had become a national leader. Many people gave thanks to the man who was working to bring them equal rights.

STRIDING TOWARD FREEDOM

The country had been watching Montgomery, Alabama, during the boycott. African Americans in other southern states began talking about what

THE LITTLE ROCK NINE

Desegregation of public schools took a long time. Brave African American students walked into hostile school environments in the South. Among the most famous group was the Little Rock Nine. These nine African American students enrolled in Central High School in Little Rock, Arkansas, in 1957. Many of the school's white students called them names, threw things at them, and even beat them. Nevertheless, the group kept going to classes. All but one graduated. (One member was expelled for answering back to an insult.)

could be done to fight racial segregation where they lived. On January 9, 1957, King and Abernathy drove to Atlanta, Georgia, to meet with African American leaders from other southern states. During the meeting, sixty African American ministers formed what came to be called the Southern Christian Leadership Conference.

Martin Luther King was elected president of the SCLC at a February 14 meeting in New Orleans, Louisiana. The SCLC wanted to start a civil rights movement in the entire South. At the New Orleans meeting, African American leaders asked President Dwight D. Eisenhower to call a conference on civil rights. Eisenhower refused.

In response, the SCLC planned a prayer march for May 17, 1957, in Washington, D.C. The march drew so much attention that hundreds of white students, teachers, and other professionals joined it. Movie stars, singers, and senators were there. They marched down Washington's Mall (a large courtyard lined by important government buildings, monuments, and museums) singing "The Battle Hymn of the Republic" and carrying signs that called for freedom and equal rights.

The huge crowd circled the Lincoln Memorial. Some of the marchers sat on the grass and unpacked picnic lunches. Martin Luther King gave a speech as he stood before the marble statue of Abraham Lincoln,

IT'S A FACT!

The lyrics of (words to) "The Battle Hymn of the Republic" date from the Civil War. But the tune is a little bit older. While the soldiers marched, they liked to come up with new lyrics to old tunes. Often the lyrics made fun of people. Julia Ward Howe, an activist and reformer, heard a version she thought was disrespectful. She wrote new lyrics that she thought were more appropriate.

King speaks to thousands of civil rights demonstrators at the Lincoln Memorial in Washington, D.C., in 1957.

the president who had proclaimed freedom
for African American slaves in the 1860s.

Soon after the prayer march, the National
Association for the Advancement of Colored
People awarded King the Spingarn Medal for his
contribution to race relations. He was the youngest
person to receive that honor. Howard University, the
Theological Seminary of the University of Chicago,

and Morehouse College–three major African American institutions of higher learning–each presented him with honorary degrees soon after.

King spent a great deal of time traveling to give speeches and attend meetings. He did get home in October 1957 when his second child, Martin Luther King III (Little Marty), was born. One night, while he was home, Coretta noticed Martin making notes of the day's events. She asked him what he was doing. He told her that he was writing a book about the bus boycotts. The title was to be *Stride toward Freedom.*

ARRESTED AND ATTACKED

On September 3, 1958, Martin and Coretta went with Abernathy to a Montgomery courtroom, where Abernathy was to testify against a man who had attacked him. At the courtroom door, a police officer refused to let King enter the room. When he asked if he could speak with Abernathy's lawyer, the officer told him that he had to leave. At that point, two officers grabbed King and twisted his arm. They led him to the police station and charged him with loitering (staying in an area for no reason) and failing to obey an officer.

Twisting King's arm behind him, police officers arrest King on September 3, 1958.

King's punishment was ten dollars or fourteen days in jail. He chose to go to jail. When Police Commissioner Sellers heard of the sentence, he paid the fine himself. He was furious. He knew King would want the publicity.

A short time later, *Stride toward Freedom* was published, and King traveled across the country to talk about the book. One day, while he was signing books in a department store in Harlem, New York, a disturbed African American woman pushed her way through the crowd and stood near him. She told him that she'd been after him for five years.

Then she took a sharp letter opener and shoved it into his chest.

King was rushed to the hospital, where surgeons removed one of his ribs and part of his breastbone. A doctor there told him that if he had sneezed, he might have drowned in his own blood.

News of King's stabbing traveled across the country. Radio and television stations broadcast hourly updates on his condition. President Eisenhower and other heads of states sent telegrams and letters to the hospital. But King's favorite letter came from someone who wasn't famous. A young girl wrote a letter saying that she'd heard that King would have died if he had sneezed. She said she was glad he didn't sneeze.

IT'S A FACT!

The doctors operating on King had to be very careful. The tip of the letter opener was touching his aorta (a tubelike channel that carries blood to the heart). If the tip had gone in any deeper, he could easily have bled to death.

CHAPTER 4
WE SHALL OVERCOME

IN THE WEEKS THAT FOLLOWED his stabbing, King had time to rest and be alone. He thought about his work, his goals, and his fight for civil rights. He thought more about Mohandas Gandhi. He tried to figure out how Gandhi's ideas could be put to work for civil rights in the United States. Soon King was well enough to leave the hospital, but his doctors told him to take it easy until he regained his strength. King listened to his doctors and decided to use the time to do something different.

A year earlier, King had received an invitation from the Gandhi Peace Foundation to visit India and to learn more about nonviolent methods.

This was a perfect time to accept the invitation. The Kings went to India in 1959.

Martin and Coretta spent a month in India. Martin spoke to large audiences about the bus boycott. Coretta sang for the crowds. He learned more about Gandhi from Indian leaders and teachers. He saw how faithful the people were to Gandhi's teaching. It made him even more committed to using nonviolent methods in the United States.

Martin and Coretta returned to the United States on March 10, 1959. Martin was ready to take his beliefs one step further. During the bus boycott, people had protested segregation by not riding city buses. They had not broken any laws. The bus boycott was an example of passive resistance. After his trip to India, King realized that passive resistance wasn't enough. He was ready to ask African Americans to disobey some unfair laws, a method called civil disobedience.

In November 1959, the Kings moved from Montgomery, Alabama, to Atlanta, Georgia, where the SCLC headquarters was located. There, King joined his father as assistant pastor at Ebenezer Baptist Church. Martin began talking about the power of peaceful civil disobedience. Young people in the South heard his message.

CIVIL DISOBEDIENCE

On January 31, 1960, Joseph McNeil, an African American student, entered a Woolworth's store in Greensboro, North Carolina and sat at its lunch counter. The waiter looked at him and said that he couldn't eat there. McNeil left quietly, but on his way home, his heart pounded and his anger grew. Sitting on the edge of his bed, he told the story to his roommate. They talked until late at night, telling each other about past discrimination. They believed that Martin Luther King was right about civil disobedience. Something had to be done. They decided to return to the counter the next day.

IT'S A FACT!
The sit-in in Greensboro, North Carolina, lasted five months. Eventually, Woolworth's desegregated its lunch counter.

They walked into the store, promising themselves to hold only a quiet demonstration. Together, they sat at the counter. Again, the waiter told them that they couldn't eat there. McNeil and

From left to right, seated: Joseph McNeil, Franklin McCain, Billy Smith, and Clarence Henderson. It is the second day of a 1960 sit-in at a segregated Woolworth's lunch counter in Greensboro, North Carolina.

his roommate sat at the counter all day. Their action was called a sit-in. The following morning, two more students joined them. Within two weeks, many students in North Carolina heard about the sit-ins. They also began to demand service in whites-only restaurants. Three months later, nonviolent sit-ins had spread to more than fifty southern cities.

In Nashville, Tennessee, Jim Lawson and about five hundred students from Fisk University marched to different lunch counters. They sang "We Shall Overcome," a popular song during the civil rights movement. The protesters were polite.

They practiced Martin Luther King's ideas about
nonviolence. They followed their own strict rules.
They dressed well. They sat up straight at the lunch
counters. Sometimes people called the students
names, poured ketchup or mustard on them, or
pushed them off the stools. Often the students were
arrested. But no matter what happened, the
protesters remained nonviolent.

While the sit-ins were becoming more popular
across the South, the King family continued to
grow. On January 30, 1961, the Kings' third child,
Dexter Scott, was born.

John F. Kennedy had become the new
president of the United States ten days earlier. At
first, leaders of the civil rights movement were
excited about the new president. But King soon felt
that Kennedy did not fully understand how bad
segregation was. With or without help from the
U.S. government in Washington, D.C., however, the
movement would go on. King and his associates
were not about to stop what they had started.

FREEDOM RIDERS

In March 1961, some students who had been
participating in sit-ins decided to test a Supreme

Court decision. Earlier that year, the Court had ruled that segregation in all areas of public transportation—not just buses—was illegal.

The students, called Freedom Riders, planned to ride buses through the South to show that segregation was still in force. They wanted the nation to see that the Supreme Court decision was being ignored. The Freedom Riders included African Americans as well as whites.

King was in Washington, D.C., on May 4 when the first riders climbed aboard the two Freedom Rider buses. He shook their hands and hugged them. As the buses pulled away, he wondered what would happen to the brave young people.

IT'S A FACT!

The Court's decision was called *Boynton v. Virginia* (1960). Bruce Boynton, an African American, had been refused service at a lunch counter in a bus terminal in Virginia. Buses that came and went from this terminal crossed state borders. The Court's decision said that public places in interstate transportation facilities could not be segregated.

CIVIL RIGHTS ORGANIZATIONS

Several other civil rights organizations were involved in the movement of the 1950s and 1960s. Some—like the Student Nonviolent Coordinating Committee (SNCC)—grew out of the sit-ins. Others, such as the Congress of Racial Equality (CORE), had been in place for a while.

James Farmer, George Houser, and other students at the University of Chicago had founded CORE in the early 1940s. They organized the Freedom Riders to test interstate desegregation at bus terminals. African American riders would use whites-only facilities. White Freedom Riders would use facilities set aside for African Americans. The riders' journey would take them from Washington, D.C., to New Orleans, Louisiana.

The buses rolled down the highway, traveling safely through Virginia. But in South Carolina, they met trouble. The buses stopped at Rock Hill, where the riders got off and walked to a white waiting room. There, a group of angry white men attacked them and knocked them to the floor. The riders looked to the police, who were standing nearby, for help, but the police just stood with their arms folded.

On Mother's Day, May 14, 1961, the two buses carrying the Freedom Riders arrived in Alabama. Just outside Anniston, an armed mob surrounded the first bus. The mob smashed windows, popped tires, and tossed a firebomb inside. As the driver

and the Freedom Riders tried to escape from the
burning bus, many were attacked and beaten.
The second bus raced on to Birmingham, Alabama,
where another gang was waiting. The Freedom
Riders were attacked. Two of them, James Person,
an African American man, and James Peck, a white
man, were brutally beaten while the police watched.
Peck's face required fifty-three stitches. Both bus
drivers quit their jobs. The bus companies refused
to allow the buses to continue to Montgomery.
The riders had to stop their ride and fly home.

**Dazed Freedom Riders watch as their bus burns outside of
Anniston, Alabama, in 1961.**

However, another group of Freedom Riders boarded a bus in Nashville, Tennessee, and headed for Montgomery, Alabama, so the journey could continue. They were singing "We Shall Overcome" as the bus crept slowly down the quiet streets of Montgomery. There were no crowds, no patrol cars, no police. But when the bus pulled into the terminal, a crowd of several hundred angry white people was there to meet them.

The crowd was armed with weapons including baseball bats, iron pipes, and chains. Both white and African American Freedom Riders were attacked. James Zwerg, a white student from Wisconsin, and John Seigenthaler, who was sent by President Kennedy to observe the situation, were beaten until they were unconscious. The violence continued for about twenty minutes before the police appeared, but no arrests were made. When a reporter asked Police Commissioner L. B. Sullivan if he had called for an ambulance, Sullivan reported that all of the town's ambulances were broken.

TRYING TO KEEP THINGS CALM

In Atlanta, King saw the ugly scene on television. He immediately flew to Montgomery. The next evening, he spoke at a crowded mass meeting at Ralph Abernathy's First Baptist Church. A white mob gathered outside. Eventually, about four thousand angry people surrounded the building. They burned a car and threw rocks and bottles through the windows. Inside the church, a low voice calmly sang.

Afraid of what might happen next, King hurried to the basement and called Robert Kennedy. He was not only the president's brother. He was the U.S. attorney general, the government's top law enforcement official. After hearing what King had to say, Kennedy told him that federal marshals, or police, were on the way. Six hundred federal marshals soon came to the scene, but there were not enough of them to control the crowd.

Attorney General Kennedy called the governor of Alabama, John Patterson, and told him he had a choice. Either he could provide protection for the people inside the church or President Kennedy would call the National Guard to take care of the problem. The governor called out about three hundred troops, and the federal marshals tossed tear gas bombs into the mob. It was late that night when the crowd finally went home. People inside the church joined hands and sang.

5

THE BATTLE FOR FREEDOM

RACISM IN BIRMINGHAM, Alabama, was even worse than in many parts of the South. King and other civil rights leaders decided to organize demonstrations there. Demonstrators needed careful training to avoid violence. King knew the effort would need strong leadership, organization, and determination.

In the spring of 1963, hundreds of demonstrators came to Birmingham to protest segregation. At first, the civil rights demonstrations were unusual because the police, under the command of Commissioner Eugene "Bull" Connor, were oddly polite. Connor was a racist, and he wasn't afraid to use violence. This time, however,

his police did not use violence against the
marchers. They only asked the demonstrators to
show parade permits for marching. The
demonstrators had no permits and were arrested.

After a few days, Bull Connor became
impatient. Hundreds of protesters were in the
Birmingham jail, but more marchers kept arriving.
Also, as the demonstrators were released from jail,
they returned to march again. Connor was seeing
the same faces over and over. A judge issued an
order to stop the SCLC and the marchers from
demonstrating. But with King's support, the
demonstrations continued.

On April 12, 1963, a bright, sunny day, King
led fifty marchers to downtown Birmingham. As he
turned around, they waved to him. They clapped
their hands and sang as they moved closer and
closer to the line of police that blocked the street.

The police were everywhere—on foot, on
motorcycles, in patrol cars, and standing on rooftops
with guns. When King and Abernathy came face-to-
face with Bull Connor, they knelt down in prayer.
On Connor's order, the police grabbed the
marchers and threw them into police vans. Sirens
howled as the vans sped toward the jail.

IT'S A FACT!

While in jail, King wrote "Letter from Birmingham Jail." He wasn't given any paper, so he wrote on scraps and in the margins of newspapers. The letter talked about his view of nonviolent protest. It said that people would only stop oppressing others if they were forced to. But he declared that the movement should not use wrong or violent methods, even to gain right or moral goals.

King was locked in a dark cell by himself. He was not allowed to use the telephone or see a lawyer. Coretta, who had given birth to their fourth child Bernice Albertine on March 28, worried about her husband's safety. A few days later, a lawyer got the other demonstrators out of jail, but King remained.

New demonstrators arrived in Birmingham. The demonstrators continued to march, get arrested, and get released each day. And each day, the Birmingham police treated them more and more harshly. Newly elected Alabama governor George Wallace set an example by supporting segregation, despite the Supreme Court's ruling against it.

King is arrested during a civil rights march in Birmingham, Alabama, in 1963. While in jail, King wrote a letter to fellow religious leaders. "Letter from Birmingham Jail" explained why racism had to be stopped.

PROBLEMS GROW

Finally, on Saturday, April 20, King was released from jail. The movement needed his leadership. It also was looking for a new strategy. Some of the leaders wanted to use children in the civil rights marches, but King was uncertain. He didn't want children to get hurt.

On May 2, about one thousand boys and girls gathered at the Sixteenth Street Baptist Church in Birmingham. Small groups of ten to fifty children marched to the center of town. They came, wave upon wave, singing and clapping. Many were arrested. The police ran out of vans to transport them, and the jails were filled. The next day, thousands more children and their parents gathered at the church.

As they marched, shouting, "We want freedom," the firefighters held heavy hoses and policemen hung on to dogs that strained at their leashes. Finally, Connor signaled for the firefighters

Under order of Commissioner Bull Connor, firefighters turn their high-pressure hoses on student protesters in Birmingham, Alabama, in May 1963. The nation watched in horror.

to turn on their hoses. Columns of water crashed into the children, knocking them down, ripping their clothes, shoving them against the sides of buildings, and driving them, bleeding and crying, into a nearby park. African American bystanders, who had not been trained in the techniques of nonviolence, became angry and hurled bricks and bottles at the firefighters. Then the police commissioner ordered the dogs to be unleashed. The animals charged, snarling and biting. The young marchers rolled on the ground as the dogs bit into their arms and legs. Torn and beaten, some of the marchers returned to the church. Hundreds of others went to jail.

Pictures of the violence appeared in newspapers and on television screens around the world. The violence of Birmingham's police became a scandal. King had public opinion on his side. By Friday, May 10, Birmingham had agreed to end segregation of lunch counters, restrooms, fitting rooms, and drinking fountains within ninety days. White businesses promised to hire African American people and improve their jobs in stores and factories. Officials agreed to cooperate with lawyers who were working for the release of jailed protesters.

On Saturday, the day after the agreement, some angry white people bombed the Gaston Hotel, where King had stayed during the demonstrations. In response, angry African American people filled the streets. They stabbed a police officer and overturned taxis. Cars, stores, and two apartment houses were burned. By Sunday morning, peace had been restored. King, who had gone home to Atlanta, returned to Birmingham to continue his call for nonviolence. To reach the young men in the community, he set out on a "pool room pilgrimage." King and Abernathy went into Birmingham bars and pool halls. They asked young African American men to give nonviolent methods a chance. Once again, King was successful. Many young men pulled knives from their belts and handed them to him. Others gave up their guns.

KING'S DREAM

In June, President Kennedy asked the U.S. Congress to pass new civil rights laws that would give equal justice and opportunity to everyone in the United States. Fourteen important civic, religious, and labor organizations planned a demonstration in Washington, D.C., to call attention

Thousands of civil rights protesters make their way to the Lincoln Memorial in Washington, D.C., during the March on Washington on August 29, 1963. King *(fourth from left)* spoke of his dream for the movement and the nation that day.

to the call for civil rights. They thought the demonstration would help gain support for equal justice from all over the country. The planners hoped that at least 100,000 people would take part.

On the morning of August 29, 1963, 250,00 people, blacks and whites, gathered for the historic March on Washington. The group marched from the Washington Monument to the Lincoln Memorial, where they listened to many speakers and entertainers. Martin Luther King Jr. was the last person to speak on that hot day.

People were tired of listening to speeches. But when King was introduced, the crowd burst into applause. Wearing a dark suit and feeling a bit nervous, King stepped to the podium. He looked out at the people. Finally, they became silent as he began his speech, one of the most memorable speeches in history. In it, he said that he had a dream that one day people would be judged not by the color of their skin, but by how they behaved toward others. He ended the speech by calling for freedom for all people.

But freedom was yet to be won for many. Sunday, September 15, was also a hot day. In Birmingham, Alabama, as children attended their Sunday school classes at the Sixteenth Street Baptist Church, someone threw a package through one of the open windows. Seconds later, the package, which contained sticks of dynamite, exploded.

IT'S A FACT!

King called 1963 the year of assassinations. In June, Medgar Evers, an NAACP leader, was shot in front of his house in Mississippi. The children at the Sixteenth Street Baptist Church died in September. Kennedy was killed in November.

Police and fire officials look into the bombing of the Sixteenth Street Baptist Church in Birmingham, Alabama, in September 1963. Four African American girls died in the bombing.

Four girls were killed, and many more children were badly injured.

On November 22, 1963, President Kennedy was killed in Dallas, Texas. The nation, as well as the rest of the world, grieved. There were also threats on King's life. He told Coretta that he didn't think he'd live to be forty.

After Kennedy was killed, Vice President Lyndon B. Johnson, a southerner, became president. Congress quickly passed the Civil Rights Act of 1964, calling for equal treatment for all races.

On July 2, King and other African American leaders watched as President Johnson signed the bill in the White House. Over national radio and television, Johnson said that all Americans were now equal.

Even though the Civil Rights Act passed, King was discouraged with the slow progress of the movement. On October 14, he was in the hospital suffering from exhaustion when he learned that he had won the Nobel Peace Prize. It is a prize awarded to people who have made valuable contributions to the good of humanity. Congratulations came from all over the world.

Although African American people had made great strides toward freedom, they still had a long way to go. They were not really free yet. King believed the next step was to ensure their right to vote.

CHAPTER 6
CROSSING THE BRIDGE

IF KING'S DREAM was going to become a reality, and if African American people were going to gain the right to vote, then voter registration was the next step. The year 1965 began with a campaign to register voters in Alabama's "Black Belt," an area heavily populated with African American people. The campaign started in Selma, Alabama. African Americans outnumbered white people in Selma but represented only 1 percent of the voters. Out of 15,000 African American people, only 350 were registered to vote. King spoke to a crowd at Brown's Chapel Methodist Church. He told them they were going to show their power through the vote.

On January 18, hundreds of people marched to the courthouse to register to vote. While they patiently stood outside, Sheriff Jim Clark, a big man who was good at maintaining Selma's racist policies, met the group. He called them names and tried to scare them.

The marches during January and February resulted in hundreds of arrests. Protesters stood for hours in front of the courthouse. Often Clark

shouted at them through a bullhorn. Sometimes they were told that the office of the registrar was closed. Other times, a few African Americans were allowed to fill out applications, but then the

Police arrest an African American man outside the Selma, Alabama, courthouse in January 1965. Charged with loitering, he had been protesting for his voter registration rights.

applications were crumpled up and tossed into the wastebasket. Sometimes people were asked very difficult or confusing questions that they couldn't answer.

At the beginning of February, King and Abernathy again planned to lead marchers from Brown's Chapel to the courthouse. The marchers had walked only three blocks when Wilson Baker, the new director of the city police, stopped them. Baker didn't like brutality, but he was willing to use it in some situations. He told the group that they were breaking the law and would have to break up. King disagreed, and Baker had the marchers arrested. The arrest of the Nobel Prize winner made headlines in newspapers around the world.

BLOODY SUNDAY

In February 1965, Jimmie Lee Jackson, his mother, and his grandfather were marching peacefully for voter registration in Selma, Alabama. Alabama state troopers were on hand with clubs and other weapons. When Jimmie saw his relatives being beaten with clubs, he tried to protect them. A state trooper shot him in the stomach, and Jimmie died days later.

Many people throughout the country were outraged by Jackson's murder. King wanted to direct these strong feelings into some positive action. He organized a march from Selma to Montgomery, the capital of Alabama. The people wanted to bring their case to Governor George Wallace, the segregationist leader of the state. But Wallace issued an order outlawing the march.

On Sunday, March 7, about six hundred protesters set off. As the demonstrators began their march, troopers waited on the Edmund Pettus Bridge. The troopers got into position and pulled on gas masks. Because King was home in Atlanta, Hosea Williams of SCLC and John Lewis of the Student Nonviolent Coordinating Committee (SNCC) led the march. When the marchers crossed the bridge, the state troopers gave them three minutes to turn around. Crowds of local white citizens taunted the marchers. Williams asked to talk to the troopers. They refused.

When the marchers did not turn back, the state police acted. They threw cans of tear gas and beat the marchers with nightsticks and bullwhips. Troopers rode their horses over fallen bodies. They swung at men, women, and children and shouted.

Alabama state troopers attack civil rights marchers outside of Selma on Sunday, March 7, 1965. The demonstrators were trying to march from Selma to the state capitol building in Montgomery to protest police brutality and murder.

Some of the white onlookers cheered. When the attack was over, John Lewis had a fractured skull, and many others were seriously injured.

That night, television news of the event shook the nation. It was called "Bloody Sunday." Newspapers around the world told the sad story. King was deeply moved by the tragedy.

MARCHING AGAIN

After Bloody Sunday, King announced that he would lead a march from Selma to Montgomery on

March 9. A judge gave an order for the march to be stopped. President Johnson asked King to postpone it. Finally, everyone came to an agreement. If the marchers turned back after crossing the bridge, there would be no violence. If they continued toward Montgomery, the troopers would respond with violence, as they had before.

Fifteen hundred demonstrators walked the same path from Brown's Chapel to the bridge, but this time there was no bloodshed. After crossing the

King led marchers across the Edmund Pettus Bridge toward Montgomery on March 9, 1965. Once across, King and the marchers peacefully knelt in prayer and returned to Selma.

bridge, King led the group in prayer, then told them to turn around.

One of the demonstrators was the Reverend James Reeb, a white minister from Boston. After the march, Reeb and a few other white ministers ate at a café owned by African Americans. As they left the restaurant, a voice shouted at them. Four white youths came out from the shadows and beat the ministers with clubs. They crushed Reeb's skull. An ambulance sped him to a hospital in Birmingham, where he died two days later.

Reeb's murder angered people even more. The day after the attack, seventy Catholic priests and nuns from Chicago arrived in Selma to protest the slaying. In Washington, President Johnson took a strong stand supporting the African American cause when he addressed a joint session of the U.S. Congress. While Johnson spoke, Martin Luther King sat alone in the living room of a friend and cried.

THE VOTING RIGHTS ACT

In the meantime, a federal judge ruled that the protesters had a right to march from Selma to Montgomery. Governor Wallace, who opposed the march, said he could not guarantee their protection.

King speaks to a crowd of more than twenty thousand civil rights marchers and other activists outside the Alabama state capitol building in Montgomery in March 1965.

Nevertheless, the march finally began on March 21. More than three thousand demonstrators crossed the Edmund Pettus Bridge. Days later, just outside Montgomery, more than twenty thousand people joined the march, which ended with a rally on the steps of the Alabama state capitol.

Influenced by the protesters' efforts and the dramatic march, Congress passed the Voting Rights Act. On August 6, 1965, when President Johnson signed it into law, both Martin Luther King Jr. and Rosa Parks were there. The new law got rid of poll taxes, which had to be paid in order to vote. It also got rid of reading tests and other voting rules that had been used to prevent African Americans from registering to vote. Federal examiners went into counties that were mostly African American to help people register.

PROBLEMS IN THE NORTH

During this time, King was also trying to organize people in cities outside the South to use nonviolent techniques. He traveled to New York and Boston.

VOTING RIGHTS

The Fifteenth Amendment to the U.S. Constitution says that no U.S. citizen can be prevented from voting because of his or her race. This amendment became part of the Constitution in 1870. In 1964, the Twenty-fourth Amendment to the Constitution was passed. It said that making people pay poll taxes to vote was illegal. In 1965, the Voting Rights Act put harsh penalties on people who were caught trying to prevent others from voting.

King ducks to avoid being hit by a rock near Chicago, Illinois, in 1966.

He also went to Chicago and other cities. King discovered that the North was harder to organize than the South. No signs said so, but racial discrimination was everywhere. Segregation was not part of the law, but it still happened. African Americans were only hired for certain jobs, mainly low-paying ones. Often in African American neighborhoods, city services such as housing inspection and garbage collection weren't good. Parks and recreation centers were run down. Street repairs were done carelessly, and sometimes they weren't done at all.

Many African American people in the North supported the Black Power movement. This movement included people who didn't believe that nonviolent methods were getting results fast enough. They rejected white values. Black Power leaders urged African American people to gain control of their own communities and form their own standards. Riots took place in several cities.

King rented a run-down apartment in Lawndale, an African American area on the West Side of Chicago. In July 1966, he led thousands of people in a march to City Hall to protest segregation in Chicago's public schools. Northern schools didn't officially keep African American children out of white schools. But often, African Americans weren't welcome to live anywhere except in African American neighborhoods.

IT'S A FACT!

King wasn't as effective in the North as he had been in the South. His civil rights campaigns had been tied to southern churches. But religion played a smaller role in the lives of most northern African Americans. So his influence as a well-educated minister counted for less.

Where a child lived determined which school he or she attended, so schools were in fact segregated.

King also organized tenants' unions to force landlords to repair the run-down buildings in African American neighborhoods. Rats crawled in the walls. Sometimes the plumbing didn't work, and sometimes there wasn't any heat or hot water.

The tenants' unions held rent strikes. The tenants refused to pay rent until repairs were made. Although rent strikes worked for a few thousand people, hundreds of thousands more needed to be organized, and that took time. Many African Americans in Chicago were impatient. Others felt powerless. They could vote, ride buses, and eat at lunch counters with whites. They could share waiting rooms, bathrooms, and drinking fountains. But they couldn't change their living conditions. African Americans were tired of living in the worst apartments, having the lowest-paying jobs, and sending their children to the worst schools. They were tired of waiting and tired of nonviolence.

KING'S METHODS CHALLENGED

In July 1966, frustration in Chicago's African American community reached a peak. During a very hot day, some children tried to stay cool by playing in the water spraying from a fire hydrant. But opening a fire hydrant was illegal, so the police closed it and sent the children home. Since there were no swimming pools in the area, many people thought the police action was unfair. People got angry, and soon a three-day riot started. A terrible riot had already occurred in Watts, an African American area of Los Angeles. A riot in Cleveland followed the one in Chicago.

Meanwhile, James Meredith, the African American student who had enrolled at the University of Mississippi, wanted to find out if freedom had really come to the South. He planned to walk from Memphis, Tennessee, to Jackson, Mississippi. He wanted to see firsthand if facilities were integrated. He wanted to make a private statement, without press or demonstrations. On the second day of the march, as he approached Hernando, Mississippi, there was a shotgun blast. Meredith fell to the ground, his back peppered with buckshot. But he was alive.

Soon after King heard the news, he went to Memphis. He and other civil rights leaders sat by Meredith's bed. They told him that they would continue his march. This march became a painful

IT'S A FACT!

Stokely Carmichael had taken part in sit-ins and Freedom Rides. He later helped found the Black Panthers, a group in the Black Power movement. Carmichael left the United States and lived the rest of his life in western Africa. He died in 1998.

experience for King. As the marchers moved down the highway, militant young African Americans joined them. They shouted out against nonviolent methods. As the marchers sang "We shall overcome," the new protesters sang "We shall overrun."

One of these African American leaders was Stokely Carmichael, a member of the SNCC. He didn't want white people marching with the group. Against King's wishes, Carmichael began raising his fist and shouting for black power. King was horrified because he thought the slogan gave the impression of black supremacy, which he felt would be as evil as white supremacy.

As the march went on, Carmichael and his followers became angrier and noisier. The marchers paused in Philadelphia, Mississippi, where three civil rights workers had been murdered two years earlier. King conducted a memorial service for them.

During the service, a crowd of white people encircled them and then attacked. The police didn't step in until some of the demonstrators started fighting back. Then the police moved in and broke up the fight. That night, at their campsite, someone shot at the marchers. Some African Americans who had guns shot back. King promised to return to Philadelphia again in a nonviolent march.

When the demonstrators reached Canton, Mississippi, they tried to camp on the grounds of an all-African American elementary school. The police told them to leave, but King and other protesters refused to go. State police moved in, throwing grenades and tear gas while battering marchers with whips, sticks, and gun butts. King escaped injury by jumping onto a truck.

The group later reached Jackson, Mississippi, and held a rally on the grounds of the state capitol. Thousands of people, including many famous entertainers, attended. Hundreds of National Guard soldiers with rifles stood around the grounds.

7 MARCHING FOR FREEDOM

BY 1967, emotions were running high on many important national issues. For example, people were deeply and bitterly divided over the involvement of the United States in the Vietnam War (1957–1975). People disagreed about whether U.S. troops should fight in South Vietnam. This Southeast Asian nation was fighting North Vietnam in a civil war.

Martin Luther King Jr. was very clear about where he stood on nonviolence and on the war issue. He was against the war, and his position made many people angry. They told him to stick to civil rights and not get involved in world affairs. But he was against violence anywhere. He knew that war was expensive. If the government spent lots of money on the Vietnam War, it would have less money to spend on programs to help the poor.

Although King actively protested the war, he continued to speak in support of the civil rights movement. African American militants also spoke out. The following July, African American communities in Newark, New Jersey, and Detroit, Michigan, took part in terrible riots.

King *(center)* locks arms with other demonstrators during an anti-Vietnam War protest in 1967. King saw a direct link between racism, poverty, and war.

President Johnson set up a commission, the National Advisory Commission on Civil Disorders. This group, also called the Kerner Commission, studied the causes of the riots. After months of study, the commission charged white people in the United States with racism. It predicted that the United States would end up with two separate, hostile societies if things did not change. The president did not like the report of his own commission.

IT'S A FACT!

In 1968, the Kerner Commission suggested direct action. The government should step in and see that public services, housing, and job opportunities were improved in African American neighborhoods.

Many people began to notice changes in King. He was angry. He was frustrated by the movement and disappointed with President Johnson. The issues of civil rights for poor people were no longer taking center stage. As a result, King began planning a Poor People's March to Washington. He thought the United States had forgotten about its problems. He said it was too

King meets citizens of Newark, New Jersey, while organizing the Poor People's March in 1968.

easy to overlook the poor. He said the poor had become invisible.

King thought the Poor People's March would have a big effect on Congress. He wanted guaranteed jobs for those who could work and an end to housing discrimination. He wanted integrated education to be enforced. Although King was tired and discouraged, he wanted to find a way to organize the working poor into unions.

STRIKE IN MEMPHIS

King traveled around the country, giving speeches and winning support for the Poor People's March. But trouble was brewing in Memphis, Tennessee.

Employees of the Memphis sanitation department, most of whom were African American, received low wages and were mistreated. Their hours were long, and collecting and hauling garbage was physically difficult and dirty work. The workers had no job security or insurance.

On Wednesday, January 31, 1968, driving rain drenched Memphis. After two hours of work, city officials sent the garbage workers home. On Friday, when they got their paychecks, the African American workers found less than their usual pay. They were told that the deduction was from having worked only two hours the previous Wednesday. They thought the deduction was fair until they talked to some white workers. The African American garbage workers learned that the white workers had been paid for a full day's work. The African Americans had been treated unfairly. Money wasn't the main issue. Racism was.

Henry Loeb, the white mayor of Memphis, refused to listen to the complaints of the workers. On February 12, they declared a strike. Mayor Loeb told the strikers that they would lose their jobs. He didn't think the strike would last, but he didn't understand how angry the people had become.

The sanitation workers stayed home while the trash piled up in people's yards. The people of Memphis begged their elected officials to do something. But the officials refused to talk to the striking workers. Instead, police brought other workers to collect the garbage from white neighborhoods.

KING COMES TO MEMPHIS

James Lawson, King's old friend from the early marches in Alabama, marched in support of the strikers. The march was peaceful until the police broke it up. Lawson called King, who was in Mississippi organizing his Poor People's March. He explained the dangerous situation in Memphis and asked King to come for a rally. King agreed to make the trip. He thought the strike in Memphis was a good example of what the Poor People's March was all about.

King was moved by the enthusiasm of the crowd at the rally. The audience sang and clapped their hands. When he spoke, King felt filled with fire as he had at the beginning of the movement. He called for all African Americans in Memphis to boycott their jobs for one day and to join in a massive march.

Thrilled by the support and enthusiasm he had seen, King decided to lead the march himself. He made this decision without knowing that there were Black Power supporters in the city. He felt so safe in Memphis that when he left the city, he didn't leave any of his aides behind to organize the nonviolent march.

IT'S A FACT!

A week before the Memphis march, a man called radio station WHBQ in Memphis. He warned that if King returned to the city, he would be shot.

On Thursday morning, March 28, about six thousand demonstrators gathered in downtown Memphis. The march was supposed to begin at 9:00 A.M. The day began hot, and it grew hotter. Many young African Americans were armed with sticks and carried signs that said "Black Power." They shuffled back and forth, asking each other where King was. As time passed, they grew more and more impatient.

By the time King's plane had landed and he had arrived at the temple, the crowd was threatening to begin the march without him. He waved to the crowd, as he hurried to the front of

King *(front right)* joins other marchers in Memphis, Tennessee, to protest unfair labor practices there in March 1968.

the line and started the march. He linked arms with the marchers on either side of him. The marchers had only gone three blocks when King heard a crash. He turned to see youths breaking windows and looting. He immediately shouted to call off the march.

The police had been parked in squad cars on nearby streets. They quickly moved in, and fighting started. The situation suddenly became dangerous, and Lawson feared for King's life. King was taken to a motel. He sat on the edge of the bed and held his head. He said that he would return in two weeks for a peaceful march.

CHAPTER 8

FREE AT LAST

(Above) King **(right center)** stands at the balcony outside his room at the Lorraine Motel in Memphis, Tennessee, on April 3, 1968.

WHILE KING WAS TALKING about peace and nonviolence, James Earl Ray was planning. He had escaped from Jefferson City Prison in Missouri in 1967 and had made his way to Birmingham. He armed himself with a powerful rifle and, on April 3, 1968, drove his car from Birmingham to Memphis. By this time, King was back in Memphis and was staying at the Lorraine Motel. Later that day, a friend of King's warned him that his life was in danger.

A crowd of about two-thousand people listens to King as he speaks about unfair labor practices in Memphis, Tennessee, on April 3, 1968.

In the evening, King spoke before a large audience. When he walked to the podium, the crowd grew quiet. The people listened as he talked about the events of the civil rights movement, his struggle, and his heartbreak at the violence. He knew there were difficult days ahead, but he had faith that everyone would be free at last. It was one of King's greatest moments, and the audience cheered loudly.

KING'S LAST DAY

By the next day, Thursday, April 4, tension was building in Memphis. Hate literature had been slipped under doors where white families lived. The White Citizens Council held a membership drive, and the Ku Klux Klan threatened to take to the streets if King marched.

At the Lorraine Motel, King and Ralph Abernathy had lunch and chatted with Martin's younger brother, A.D. The brothers then called their mother to share their high spirits for the march to come.

That same afternoon, James Earl Ray checked into a shabby rooming house near the motel. The bathroom was at the end of the hall. From there, Ray had an almost perfect view of the Lorraine Motel.

In room 306 of the Lorraine, King was getting ready to go to dinner at the home of the Reverend Samuel B. Kyles. A limousine waited below to pick up King and his group. King was in a happy mood. Abernathy wasn't quite ready, so King stood waiting

with Kyles at the iron railing along the motel
balcony. Two young SCLC activists, Andrew Young
and Jesse Jackson, were also on hand.

THE FINAL MOMENTS

A few minutes later, Kyles walked down to the
parking lot. King stood alone at the iron railing.
Still in the room, Abernathy was standing in front
of the mirror with aftershave lotion in his palms.
He was just lifting his hands up to his face when he
heard a pop like a firecracker. A bullet had hit
Martin Luther King Jr. so forcefully that it had
knocked him backward.

A nearby undercover police officer hurried to
King's side. He tried to stop the flow of blood by
pressing a towel against the wound. The bullet had
torn away the right side of King's face and neck.
King tried to speak, but only a faint murmur came
from his mouth. Abernathy thought his friend was
telling him that he'd expected this to happen.
Andrew Young fell to his knees to see if he could
find a pulse. He thought he found a faint beat.

A patrolman who had been watching the motel
from the nearby fire station heard the shot and saw
King fall. The fire captain called for an ambulance.

King lies wounded *(center)* outside his motel room on April 4, 1968. Friends and fellow activists point in the direction of the gunshot they heard.

Minutes later, the ambulance screeched into the courtyard. At the hospital, Ralph Abernathy walked beside the stretcher as King arrived at the emergency room. It pained Abernathy to see his friend suddenly look so small and helpless.

The doctors and nurses worked quickly under bright lights. They tried to save King's life, but the bullet had done too much damage. His heartbeat began to fade. His heart beat slowed, until finally, it stopped.

Martin Luther King Jr., who had based his life on the practice of nonviolence, was dead. Outside the emergency room, Ralph Abernathy led a small group of friends in prayer.

HONORING DR. KING

People all over the world told of their sorrow at King's death. President Johnson declared Sunday, April 7, a national day of mourning. All flags on U.S. government buildings flew at half-mast.

On Monday, April 8, the Memphis march that King had planned to lead took place. Coretta and three of the King children joined Ralph Abernathy. Together, they led thirty thousand people in the memorial march. Ten days later, the sanitation workers won a settlement that improved their wages and benefits.

After the Memphis march, King's body was taken home to Atlanta, where it lay in the chapel at Spelman College. More than a thousand mourners filed by each hour to pay their final respects. Vice President Hubert H. Humphrey was there. King's funeral drew members of Congress, mayors of major U.S. cities, and foreign leaders. Eight hundred people squeezed into Ebenezer Baptist

Church. But almost one hundred thousand more gathered outside.

After the church service, the pallbearers placed Martin Luther King's casket in a farm cart drawn by mules for his final march. A procession of mourners followed in the slow, sad walk to Morehouse College, where a public ceremony was held. King's body was then laid to rest in Southview Cemetery. The inscription on his

Two mules pull a cart carrying King's coffin through the streets of Atlanta, Georgia, on April 9, 1968. Thousands of mourners attended his funeral that day.

monument reads: "Free at Last, Free at Last, Thank God Almighty, I'm Free at Last."

AFTERMATH

People were sad and angry about the killing. While hundreds of thousands of people cried and promised to keep King's dream alive, others burned and looted. Riots started in more than one hundred cities. Federal troops and the National Guard were called in. After working most of his life for nonviolence, King's death had started a whole new wave of violence.

James Earl Ray was captured at Heathrow Airport in London,

A young woman is saddened by the death of Martin Luther King Jr. Much of the nation mourned with her for the loss of the respected activist.

JAMES EARL RAY

For many years, Ray tried to get a new trial. He suggested that the U.S. government had covered up the real people who'd planned King's assassination. In 1997, Ray met with Dexter King, Dr. King's son. At that meeting, he declared that he had not killed Dexter's father. After this meeting, the King family joined Ray's family in calling for a new trial. They felt it would be the only way to discover the truth. Ray died in 1998. No new trial was ever held.

England, two months after he shot King. He pleaded guilty to murder and was sentenced to ninety-nine years in prison. However, many questions about the killing remain unanswered, and many people believe that Ray did not act alone. They think that he was only a small part of a larger plan.

Ralph Abernathy fulfilled King's wish for a Poor People's March on Washington. In May 1968, he led the march to show politicians the problems faced by poor people living in a wealthy country. King asked why millions of people suffered from poverty in a nation of such wealth.

Martin Luther King Jr. did not solve all the problems of racism and war and poverty, but he led the way toward peace, justice, and equality for all.

He didn't have all the answers. No one does. But he had faith that people were basically good, and he had hope for the future. Perhaps even more important, he shared his faith and hope. He led people to see the world as it might be and to believe that, working together, they could change it.

In 1963, fewer than fifty African Americans held political office in the South. More than forty years later, hundreds of African American men and women hold political office. Major U.S. cities–including Atlanta, Chicago, Los Angeles, and New York–have elected African American mayors. African Americans are members of Congress and of state legislatures.

Martin Luther King was a great leader. To honor him, Congress declared King's birthday a national holiday to be celebrated on the third Monday of January. The memory of Martin Luther King Jr. lives on, and the work that he began continues.

GLOSSARY

Black Power: the slogan of militant African Americans; the use of the political and economic power of African Americans, usually to promote racial equality

boycott: the refusal to deal with a business or organization in order to express disapproval or force change

civil disobedience: the refusal to obey laws viewed as immoral and accepting punishment for breaking such laws

civil rights: the rights of personal liberty guaranteed by law

desegregate: to stop the practice of separating people according to age, race, gender, or other factors

discrimination: the act of treating a person or group differently from others based on age, race, gender, or other factors

Freedom Riders: civil rights workers who rode through southern states during the 1960s to see if public facilities such as bus stations had been desegregated

ghetto: a usually poor section of a city where often people of the same race and ethnicity live

integrate: to end segregation and bring about equality under the law

Ku Klux Klan: a racist terrorist organization that uses misinformation, threats, and violence to further white power

militant: aggressive or engaged in warfare

National Association for the Advancement of Colored People (NAACP): a U.S. civil rights organization that works to end discrimination against African Americans and other minority groups

nonviolence: the act of purposefully choosing not to use violence

racism: a false belief that one race is superior to another

segregation: the separation of one group of people from another based on race or ethnic background

sit-in: an act of civil disobedience where demonstrators sit down at a targeted place and refuse to leave until an unfair law, policy, or rule is changed. During the civil rights movement, people held sit-ins at racially segregated businesses to protest discrimination and segregation.

Southern Christian Leadership Conference (SCLC): a U.S. civil rights organization started during the 1950s that works to gain equal rights for African Americans and other minority groups through nonviolent civil protest and community organizing

stereotype: an opinion based on prejudiced (unfair) information about a group or a person

Student Nonviolent Coordinating Committee (SNCC): a U.S. civil rights organization that existed from 1959 to 1972. Under the leadership of Stokely Carmichael, it promoted sit-ins and Black Power.

SELECTED BIBLIOGRAPHY

Abernathy, Ralph David. *And the Walls Came Tumbling Down*. New York: Harper and Row, 1989.

Bennett, Lerone, Jr. *What Manner of Man: A Biography of Martin Luther King, Jr*. Chicago: Johnson Publishing, 1968.

Bishop, Jim. *The Days of Martin Luther King, Jr*. New York: G. P. Putnam's Sons, 1971.

Branch, Taylor. *Parting the Waters: America in the King Years, 1954–63*. New York: Simon and Schuster, 1988.

Clayton, Edward T. *Martin Luther King: The Peaceful Warrior*. Englewood Cliffs, NJ: Prentice-Hall, 1964.

Fairclough, Adam. *Martin Luther King, Jr*. Athens: University of Georgia Press, 1995.

Frank, Gerold. *An American Death: The True Story of the Assassination of Dr. Martin Luther King, Jr. and the Greatest Manhunt of Our Time*. Garden City, NY: Doubleday, 1972.

Haskins, James. *The Life and Death of Martin Luther King, Jr*. New York: Lothrop, Lee and Shepard, 1977.

Lewis, David L. *King: A Critical Biography*. New York: Praeger Publishers, 1970.

Oates, Stephen B. *Let the Trumpet Sound: The Life of Martin Luther King, Jr*. New York: Harper and Row Publishers, 1982.

Presston, Edward. *Martin Luther King: Fighter for Freedom*. Garden City, NY: Doubleday, 1968.

Ralph, James. *Northern Protest: Martin Luther King, Jr., Chicago, and the Civil Rights Movement*. Cambridge, MA: Harvard University Press, 1993.

Schulke, Flip, and Penelope O. McPhee. *King Remembered*. New York: W. W. Norton, 1986.

Ching, Jacqueline. *The Assassination of Martin Luther King, Jr.* New York: Rosen, 2002.

Farris, Christine King. *My Brother Martin: A Sister Remembers Growing Up with the Rev. Dr. Martin Luther King Jr.* New York: Simon and Schuster, 2003.

Finlayson, Reggie. *We Shall Overcome: The History of the American Civil Rights Movement.* Minneapolis: Lerner Publications Company, 2003.

Gogerly, Liz. *The Dream of Martin Luther King: August 28, 1963.* Austin, TX: Raintree, 2003.

The King Center.
http://www.thekingcenter.com
Founded by Coretta Scott King, The King Center in Atlanta, Georgia, is the official living memorial to Dr. King and his work.

Klingel, Cynthia Fitterer. *Coretta Scott King.* Chanhassen, MN: Child's World, 1999.

Levine, Ellen. *Freedom's Children: Young Civil Rights Activists Tell Their Own Stories.* New York: Putnam, 2000.

Manheimer, Ann S. *Martin Luther King Jr.: Dreaming of Equality.* Minneapolis: Carolrhoda Books, Inc., 2005.

The Martin Luther King Jr. Historic Site.
http://www.nps.gov/malu
The area in Atlanta where Dr. King grew up and preached has become part of the National Park Service. The website gives details for visits and ongoing programs.

McWhorter, Diane. *A Dream of Freedom: The Civil Rights Movement from 1954 to 1968.* New York: Scholastic, 2004.

The Seattle Times and Martin Luther King Jr.
http://seattletimes.nwsource.com/mlk
This site not only offers information about Dr. King but also details the events of the civil rights movement.

INDEX

PHOTO ACKNOWLEDGMENTS

Photographs are used with the permission of: Archives Collection, Birmingham Public Library, Birmingham, AL, pp. 4, 71; © Marion Post Wolcott/Library of Congress/Getty Images, p. 7; courtesy of the Library of Congress, pp. 12 (LC-USZ62-124874), 57 (LC-USZ62-118472); © Hulton Archive/Getty Images, p. 15; © Bettmann/CORBIS, pp. 18, 20, 27, 40, 42, 48, 61, 65, 66, 74, 77, 78, 80, 82, 91, 95, 98; © AP|Wide World Photos, pp. 23, 31, 97; © Don Cravens/Time Life Pictures/Getty Images, pp. 32, 35, 36, 38; National Archives, pp. 37, 69; © Paul Schutzer/Time Life Getty Images, p. 46; © *News and Record*, Jack Moebes/AP|Wide World Photos, p. 53; © AFP/Getty Images, pp. 89, 103; © Joseph Louw/Time Life Pictures/Getty Images, p. 101; © *Washington Post*: reprinted by permission of the D.C. Public Library, p. 104.

Cover: © Flip Schulke/CORBIS